Tarantula

Monica Harris

Heinemann Library
Chicago, Illinois

Designed by Ginkgo Creative, Inc.
Printed and bound in the United States by Lake Book Manufacturing, Inc.
Photo research by Scott Braut

07 06 05 04
10 9 8 7 6 5 4 3 2

Library of Congress Cataloging-in-Publication Data
Harris, Monica, 1964-
   Tarantula / Monica Harris.
       p. cm. — (Bug books)
Summary: An introduction to the physical characteristics, habits, and natural environment of the tarantula.
Includes bibliographical references (p.   ).
   ISBN: 1-40340-764-9 (HC), 1-40340-993-5 (Pbk.)
   1. Tarantulas—Juvenile literature. [1. Tarantulas. 2. Spiders.] I. Title. II. Series.
   QL458.42.T5 H37 2003
   595.4'4—dc21
                              2002004024

Acknowledgments
The author and publishers are grateful to the following for permission to reproduce copyright material:
pp. 4, 5, 10, 11, 13, 14, 15, 16, 19, 20, 22, 24, 26, 28 Rick C. West; p. 6 James H. Robinson; pp. 7, 8, 9, 25, 29 James C. Cokendolpher; p. 12 Pascal Goetgheluck/Ardea London; p. 17 Lloyd R. Brockus III/JLM Visuals; p. 18 James P. Rowan; p. 21 Frank Krahmer/Bruce Coleman Inc.; p. 23 Owen Franken/Corbis; p. 27 Andrew Syred/Science Photo Library.

Illustration, p. 30, by Will Hobbs.
Cover photograph by Rick C. West.

Every effort has been made to contact copyright holders of any material reproduced in this book. Any omissions will be rectified in subsequent printings if notice is given to the publisher.

Special thanks to Dr. William Shear, Department of Biology, Hampden-Sydney College, for his review of this book.

Some words are shown in bold, **like this**. You can find out what they mean by looking in the glossary.

Contents

What Are Tarantulas?

Tarantulas are the biggest **spiders** in the world. They are not **insects.** Insects have six legs. Spiders are **arachnids.** They have eight legs.

There are more than 800 different kinds of tarantulas. They come in many colors and sizes. Tarantulas can be brown, black, green, or even blue.

What Do Tarantulas Look Like?

A tarantula's body has two parts. The tarantula's head and chest make up the **cephalothorax.** The other part is the **abdomen.** Tarantulas have eight legs and eight eyes.

Tarantulas have thick hairs. They help the spider feel things around it. A tarantula's mouthparts have sharp **fangs.** There are two short "arms" in front. They help the spider hold things.

How Big Are Tarantulas?

Most tarantulas can fit in an **adult's** hand. **Male** tarantulas are smaller and thinner than **females.**

The biggest tarantula in the world is from South America. It is called the Goliath tarantula. It is about as big as a dinner plate. It's large enough to hunt birds!

How Are Tarantulas Born?

After **mating,** the **female** tarantula makes part of a **silk cocoon.** The silk comes from her **spinnerets.** She puts hundreds of yellow eggs in it and covers them with more silk.

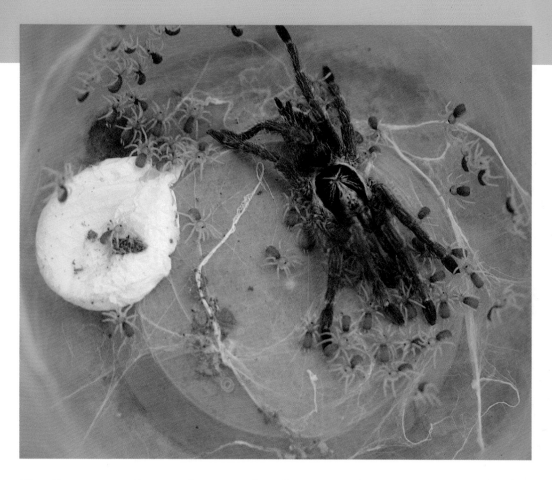

Baby spiders **hatch** from the eggs after several weeks. They bite holes in the cocoon and crawl out. Baby spiders are called **spiderlings.**

How Do Tarantulas Grow?

As a **spiderling** grows, its skin gets too small. So, it sheds the skin for a new and bigger one. This is called **molting.**

old skin

Tarantulas molt eleven to fifteen times before they are **adults. Females** become adults when they are about ten to twelve years old.

What Do Tarantulas Eat?

A tarantula is a **predator.** It hunts
for food. A tarantula will eat **insects,**
mice, frogs, and bats. It sticks the **prey**
with large **fangs.**

Fangs put **venom** into the prey. Venom stops the animal from moving. The tarantula bites the animal's body until it is mushy. Then the tarantula sucks up the food.

Which Animals Attack Tarantulas?

Toads, birds, and monkeys eat tarantulas. Tarantulas stand on their back legs when they are scared. They rub their mouthparts together. This makes a hissing noise.

Female wasps sting tarantulas and take them to their nests. They lay eggs on top of the spider. When the eggs **hatch,** the wasp **larvae** eat the tarantula.

Where Do Tarantulas Live?

Tarantulas live where it is warm. They are found in deserts, woodlands, and rain forests. They live in underground **burrows,** under logs, and in trees.

Tarantulas put **silk** threads across the opening of their burrows. The threads move if a **predator** or **prey** animal touches them. The tarantula's body hairs feel the threads move.

How Do Tarantulas Move?

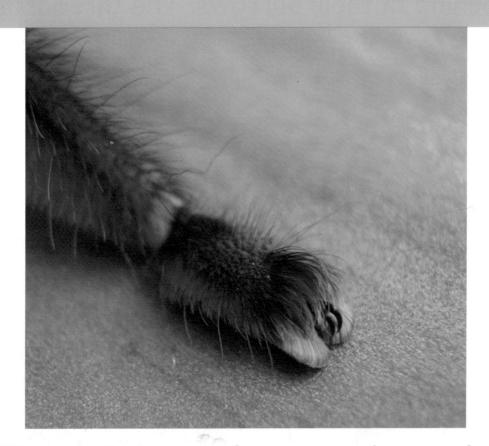

Tarantulas move fast using their eight legs. At the end of each leg is a **claw tuft.** These are hairs that help the tarantula hold onto smooth things.

Tarantulas do not move around very much. They do not have good eyesight. A tarantula sitting on your shoulder could not see past your hand.

How Long Do Tarantulas Live?

Female tarantulas can live for about 25 years. **Male** tarantulas live for five to nine years. Females sometimes eat males after **mating.**

Some tarantulas live shorter lives because of humans. They get run over by cars while crossing busy roads. Some tarantulas are eaten by people.

What Do Tarantulas Do?

Tarantulas eat **insects.** Some insects
eat a lot of plants. If tarantulas
did not eat these insects, there would
be too many.

An angry tarantula can rub its **abdomen** with its back legs. This sends stinging hairs into the air that land on the **predator.** A tarantula can get a bald spot from losing hairs.

How Are Tarantulas Special?

If a tarantula loses a leg, it can grow a new one. When the **spider** crawls out of its old skin during **molting,** the new leg is there.

Most spiders have **fangs** that point in and pinch. But tarantulas have fangs that point down. They can hold their **prey** down when they bite it.

Thinking about Tarantulas

White threads are coming out of this tarantula's **abdomen.** What are the threads?

One of these tarantulas looks dead,
but it isn't. Why does it look this way?

Tarantula Map

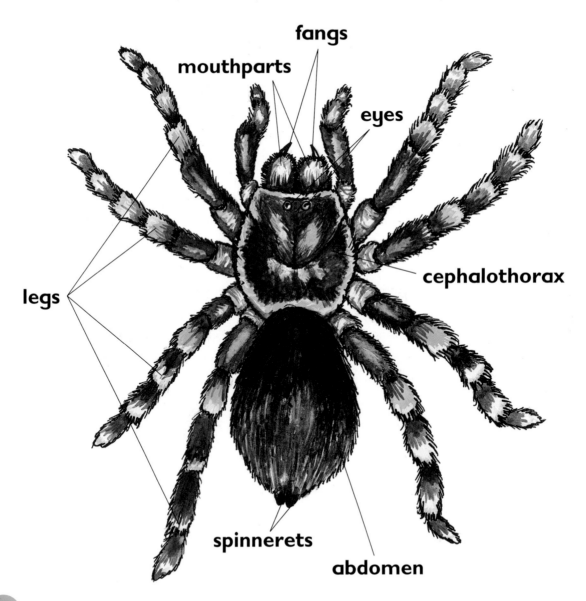

fangs

mouthparts

eyes

cephalothorax

legs

spinnerets

abdomen

Glossary

abdomen belly of an animal

adult grown-up

arachnids group of animals that includes spiders, ticks, and scorpions

burrow animal's home

cephalothorax body part that has the head and chest together

claw tuft special leg parts for holding onto things

cocoon silk bag for storing eggs

fang special mouthpart with a tube inside

female girl

hatch to come out of an egg

insect animal with six legs and three body parts

larvae baby insect. It looks like a small worm.

male boy

mate when a male and a female come together to make babies

molt get rid of skin that is too small

predator animal that hunts other animals for food

prey animal eaten by other animals

silk thin, shiny thread

spider animal with eight legs that can make silk

spiderling baby spider

spinnerets body parts that make silk

venom liquid that can harm an animal

More Books to Read

McGinty, Alice B. *Tarantula*. New York: PowerKids Press, 2002.

Murray, Julie. *Tarantula Spiders*. Minneapolis: Abdo & Daughters, 2002.

Index